THE PATH OF CHAMPIONS

JEFF RAYMOND UKAH

COPYRIGHT

Table of Contents

DEDICATION

This book is dedicated to the ministers of the Gospel Time Ministries Worldwide, and also to the youths who are yearning for greatness.

ACKNOWLEDGEMENTS

I am grateful to the editorial team of Gospel Time Publication who contributed to the development of this book: my wife, Favour O.Ukah, Donald. U. Ukah, Ebere. C. Okpara, Bro Chidi Egwuasi, Bro Cyprain Maduforo and Ihuoma Lovelyn Ofoeze.

I am highly indebted to my late mother - Nneoma Sussana Ukah, who motivated me to write this book through her life style. To my brothers - Godwin, Chukwuma and Alphonsus, who cheered me up when it seemed I`d finished, I am proud of you.

As always, Ben Iyke Onunwa, Chinedu Anunibe, Frank Osigwe deserve many thanks for their prayers as I worked on this book.

INTRODUCTION

You are not finished when you are defeated, you are finished when you quit. The devil may emphasize the magnitude of your problem under certain circumstances you find yourself in today. Some well-meaning people might even suggest that you throw in the towel. Never quit on God for He never quits on you.

There is no victory without a fight. No one becomes a champion until he has won a fight. You don't win by wishing, you win by fighting. No one excels in life outside exercise. Jesus said; *"To him that overcometh will I grant to sit with Me in My throne, even as I also overcame, and Am set down with My father in His throne"*.

There is something to overcome before you can become. You don't become until you first overcome. Even Jesus knew and passed through the same process.

Apostle Paul told us that his fight was a good fight because there's a prize for him, "A crown" (2 Timothy 4:7-8 paraphrased). He fought to win that crown. It didn't just drop on him.

"The Lord our God spoke unto us in Horeb, saying, "Ye have dwelt long enough in this mount. Turn you and take your journey, and go to the mount of the Amorites, and unto all the places nigh there unto, in the pillar, in the hills and in the valley, and on the south and by the sea sick, to the land of Canaanites, and unto Lebanon unto the great river, the river of Euphrates" (Deuteronomy 1:6-7).

God gave the land, but we will not get there until we have won the battle. Listen to this:-

"Fear not, little folk; for it is your father's good pleasure to give you the kingdom". –
Luke 12:32

"And from the days of John the Baptist until now, the kingdom of heaven suffereth violence. And the violent taketh it by force". – Matthew 11:12

This seems like paradox but Jesus is saying that the enemy is tirelessly working to deny you your heritage but He encouraged us not to give up.

Nothing in life comes easy. Even the children of Israel had to walk in the wilderness for forty years before they got to the Promised Land.

Difficulties are simply 'opportunities' in disguise to help you cultivate the virtues of patience. The only success outside hard work is the dictionary definition of success. Practical experience is acquired through concurrent field work and not just by vision". Manna fell but the children of Israel had to gather it before they could eat. As you know, God will provide you with shovel, but you have to do the digging".

Winston Churchill's short and profound speech at his alma-mater was '' Never, never, never, never give up". Nobody will have a second chance to make the first impression. Life is a race and only committed runners will make the most of it. David (the shepherd boy) told his brothers that there is a cause for his coming to the battle field "No matter how big the battle, there are reasons for it. Challenges are the catalysts for our change they come to change us.

The sound of time ring at the news that another day is through. Someone slipped and fell. Was that someone you?. You may sort for added strength, your courage to renew. Do not be disheartened for I bring hope to you. It is no secret what the Lord can do. What He has done for others, He will do for you. With His hand wide open, He pardons you. It is no secret what the Lord can do.

Remember, man's extremity is God's opportunity. Therefore, rise and take the challenge. Oppositions are scaffolds to our God-ordained positions.

Chapter 1

GIANTS TO CONQUER

There are always giants to conquer before one assumes a championship position. There may be hills out there on your path to greatness, just to discourage you. They could be mockers to pull you back. Discouragement is the costliest product in devil's supermarket. Many people today get discouraged at the look of things. Nothing is as bad as its first appearance. Even the cross scared Jesus. Therefore, before one is revealed, he needs to be seriously involved, "Revelation demands your total involvement".

Every destiny in life, has a Goliath. God promised you blessings but I want to tell you that the devil (our great enemy) will not fold his hands watch you get there. He attacks with many things to intimidate you.

"And there went out a champion out of the camp of the Philistine named Goliath of Gath, whose height was six cubit and a span. And he had a helmet of brass upon his head, and he was armed with a coat nail; and the weight of the coat was five thousand shekels of brass. And he had greave of brass upon his legs, and a target of brass between his shoulders, and the staff of his spear was like a spear's head weighted six hundred shekels of iron; and one bearing a shield went before him". – 1 Samuel 17:4-7.

To every success road, there is always a detour.

"Rise ye up, take a journey and pass over the river Armon; behold, I have given into thine hand Sihonthe Amorite, king of Heshbon and his land. Begin to possess and contend with him in battle".

Deuteronomy 2:24

You can see that the appearance of this uncircumcised Philistine was so intimidating and demoralizing that the trained soldiers of Israel ran into hiding for forty days including David's elder brothers. Devil does not fear your position or title as a head pastor, usher, prayer warrior or whatever title you wear. Remember the brighter the light the darker the darkness surrounding it.

The title you wear is not as important as the task you accomplish.

"For a great door and effectual is open unto me, and there are many adversaries". I Corinthians 16:9

Apostle Paul encountered many adversaries, then who are you to escape adversity?. "Anything cheap has no value". There were likes of Saul, Eliab and Abinadab in the battle field, but only the David like-hearted won the battle. It takes the heart of a lion to have a lion share. Satan's major assignment is to see you fall, so don't neglect his existence.

MAJOR WEAPONS OF DEVIL'S ATTACK

A.   Disappointments

B.   Careless moments

C.   Fear and Doubt

D.   Blame game

Disappointment can come from any angle; it can come from one's spouse, close friends, colleagues or one's mentor. We are sometimes confronted by problems, disappointments and frustrations, but it is how we deal with our setbacks that will sharpen our lives more than anything else we do.

"Then Jezebel sent a messenger unto Elijah, saying, 'so let the gods do to me, and more also, if I make not thy life as the life of one of them by tomorrow about this time. And when he saw that, he arose and went for his life, and came to Beersheba, which belongs to Judah, and left his servant there, but him himself went a day's journey into the wilderness, and came and sat down under a Jupiter three, and he requested for himself that he might die, and said, 'it is enough', now, oh Lord take my life; for I am not better than my father". - 1Kings 19:2-4

Just by the voice of a vociferous woman called Jezebel, a brave and wonderful Prophet Elijah became discouraged and disappointed to the extent of asking God to terminate his life. All his past achievements notwithstanding.

Understand that emotions of defeat and depression may stop you from taking the very actions that can change your life. You must believe that even though things may look impossible now, you can turn them around. Depression is the trap of the enemy for captivity.

"Looking unto Jesus the author and finisher of our faith; who for the joy that was set before him endured the cross, despising the shame, and is set down at the right hand of the throne of God"

Hebrews 12:2

Management is the key to life as crisis is the child of greatness. Majority have put men on higher pedestals, making men their mini Jireh and their source of livelihood. The moment you depend on yourself or any man, God will give up on you. See the invisible (project into the future) if you want to succeed in life. Disappointment only comes if you are focusing on your immediate environment. This is a strong weapon of the devil and he doesn't change his winning strategy easily. It has pulled men and women of great caliber down. It has destroyed visions and callings of great men and women of God.

Hear this:-

"The thief cometh not, but to steal, and to kill, and to destroy"

John 10:10a.

The Bible called DISAPPOINTMENT here the THIEF. A thief is one who steals something belonging to some other person(s). Disappointment can rob you of your great ideas, relationships, marriage and businesses.

Many left their marriages today because they were disappointed by their spouse. Disappointment may seem very common and little, but very powerful at work in any life or relationship. Again, it is called in the bible little foxes that eat up the grape.

"Take us the foxes, the little foxes that spoil the vines:
for our vines have tender grapes."

Songs of Solomon 2:15

My advice to you dear reader is to take away the little foxes yourself once you notice them. This disappointment has rendered many homes motherless, fatherless, wifeless and husbandless. So you can do away with it today. You can't be thinking like a peasant and expect to enjoy in a palace.

CARELESS MOMENTS

Devil told Samson that he wants to knock him out. What is your secret? Samson shouted oh! You think you can knock me down? And he forgot that persistence and persuasion can wear any man down.

"And it came to pass afterward, that he loved a
woman in the valley of Sorek whose name was
Delilah. And the lords of the Philistines came up unto
her, and said unto her, entice him, and see wherein
his great strength lieth, and by what means we may
prevail against him, that we may bind him to afflict
him: and we will give thee every one of us eleven
hundred pieces of silver. " - Judges 16:4-5.

Samson had seven locks of anointing always guided by the spirit of God but by a single act of carelessness, he lost his anointing, eyes and life. I have heard some men and women say that it can't happen to them because they are on fire for God. I don't think you can be on a better fire than Samson or David.

"And it came to pass after the year was expired, at the time when kings go forth to battle, that David sent Joab, and his servants with him, and all Israel; and they destroyed the children of Ammon, and besieged Rabbah. But David tarried still at Jerusalem. And it came to pass in an evening tide that David arose from off his bed, and walked upon the roof of the king's house; from trhe roof he saw a woman washing herself, and the woman was very beautiful to look upon. And David sent and inquire after the woman. And one said, is not this Bathsheba the daughter of Eliam, the wife of Uriah the Hittite?. And David send messengers to her, for she was purified from her uncleanness; and she returned unto her house.

2 Samuel 11:1-4

What do you do when no one is watching? Verse 1 –

"And it came to pass after the year was expired, at the time when kings go forth to battle, that David sent Joab, and his servants with him, and all Israel; and they destroyed the children of Ammon, and besieged Rabbah. But David tarried still at Jerusalem".

The most tempting hour with most husbands and wives are hours when no one is at home with them except the house helps especially when he's handsome or she's beautiful. David was supposed to be at the war-front but he tarried at Jerusalem while other kings were outside. But David tarried still at Jerusalem and the giant not Goliath this time hunted for his life and destiny. So many will say it doesn't matter. Let me quickly tell you, it doesn't matter will soon become matters arising. Jesus applied great wisdom during his earthly ministry. He had twelve ushers, but three out of the twelve went everywhere with him. He never operated anything secret in life. Be warned! You that keep your life in key and locks. Remember, once you make this mistake like David, devil will throw discouragement on you. This has made so many lose their lives by either suicide or abortion. Some great ministries has gone today by this single act of carelessness.

What shall it profit a man if he gains the whole world and loses his own soul?.You started well, hot for the Lord but today, you have become ice water by your careless acts. Folks, no matter how far one has gone doing the wrong thing, there could still be a 'U' turn. Beware of devil's crusade. We are in the world governed by the operations of the devil. Women are being used for operation show me your breast in the name of fashion these days coupled with men in their sagging moods.   All of these are devil's operations manifested in human carelessness. Hear this:

"The words of King Lemuel, the prophecy that his mother taught him. What, my son? And what, the son of my womb? And what, the son of my vow? Give not thy strength unto women, nor thy ways to that which destroyed kings". - Prov. 31:1-3

Carelessness has killed so many great men and women. Do not be one. A wise man will hear and increase learning; and a man of understanding shall attend unto wise counsels. If the devil knows you are a strong man or woman that you will not easily yield to temptations, he will plant or provide you with either a man or woman who will sidetrack you wherever you turn, consistently presenting the same temptation over and over again. Just like water drops over rocks will reduce the hardest rock to nothing. The moment you know that this guy or fellow is not for your good, please separate yourself from him. Consider Joseph and Potiphar's wife: **"you can lose your coat and the pleasure but not your life"**. Whatever may want to kill you, kill it first. Note, the serpent Adam did not kill in Genesis became a dragon in Revelation.

<u>BLAME GAME</u>

Friends, many are fond of transferring blames to others. This is also called "The disease of me" No one wants to take the blame for any wrong.

"Many ruin their chances and blame the Lord for it, some blame the devil or their family background."
Proverbs 19: 3 (paraphrased).

Your problem is not God; your problem is distrust and doubt.

"Now there is at Jerusalem by the sheep market a pool, which is called In Hebrew tongue Bethesda, having five poachers. In these lay a great multitude of impotent folk, of blind, halt, withered, waiting for the moving of the water. For angel went down at certain season into the Pool, and troubled the water: whosoever then first after the troubling of the water stepped in was made whole of whatsoever disease he had. And a certain man was there, which had an infirmity thirty and eight Years. When Jesus saw lie, and knew that he had been now long time in that case, he said unto him, wilt thou be made whole? The impotent man answered him. Sir, I have no man, when the water is troubled to put me into the pool; but while I am coming another steppeth down before me". - John 5:2-9.

A lot of people are influenced by the Bethesda syndrome, looking for whom to shift their problems to. This man at the pool, celebrated thirty eight anniversary close to his miracle and had no thought of positioning himself in the water to wait for his miracle. He was so busy but not effective.

Your problem today is 'you', if you won't do something about it, you will remain there. The first law of motion states that actions and reactions are equal and opposite. Folks, nothing in life will be attained if all the possible odds are removed. Elijah a man used by God in several capacities, over worked himself and became tired. Due to the devil's job, he lost focus in God and regretted living.

"But he himself went a day's journey into the wilderness, and came and sat down under a juniper tree: and he requested for himself that he might die; and said, it is enough; now, o lord, take away my life; for I am not better than my Father's".

- 1 kings 19: 4.

Devil is not afraid of your title or position neither is he scared of your exploits. Your problem is not God, your problem is doubt and distrust.

"They that trust in the Lord shall be as mount Zion which cannot be removed but abided forever".

Psalms 125:1.

Your trust gives you the courage you require in any conflict of life. Don't expect a smooth ride. There are giants you must conquer to assume your God ordained position.

"Rise ye up, take your journey and pass over the river Arnon; behold, I have given into thine hand Sihon the Amorite, King of Heshbon, and his land: begin to possess it, and contend with him in battle".

Deuteronomy 2:24

It is contention that gives birth to possession. Folks, no matter the prophecy you have received from the most anointed prophet, all of these, demand your involvement. God told Abraham, that in blessing I will bless you ... But Abraham had to engage in cattle rearing business.

FEAR AND DOUBT

FEAR: Fear is false evidence appearing real. Fear is not a limitation, it is only the edge of your comfort zone. Fear is the opposite of faith. Without faith, God can never come to your aid. Faith is having an unshakeable confidence in God's own ability that he will handle your impossibilities. Fear destroys our decision, meanwhile, decision is the pathway to honor. It weakens us from acting. The fear of the giant called Goliath kept all the armies of Israel in hiding for forty days.

"And he stood and cried unto the armies of Israel, and said unto them, are you come out to set your battle in array, am not I a Philistine, and ye servant to Saul? Choose you a man for you, and let him come down to me if he be able to fight with me, and to kill me, then will we be your servant but if I prevail against him, and win him, then shall ye be our servant and serve us. And the Philistine said, I defy the armies of Israel this day; give me a man that we may fight together. When Saul and all Israel heard those words of the Philistine, they were dismayed, and greatly afraid."

1 Samuel 17: 8-11.

Many today are victims of their mouth rather than the devil. Let's take a lesson from this boy called David: He declared the end of the fight before the final whistle.

Hear this: 'The battle is the Lord's'. There is miracle in your mouth - Your mouth is the principal requirement in the school of signs and wonders. If you cannot make a sound, you cannot enjoy a sign. Your mouth is one weapon you have that the enemy wants to attack. For instance, if you are in a dream, in some cases, you find it difficult to shout Jesus in case of attacks instead you will wake up and begin to pant.

"For I will give you a mouth and wisdom, which all your adversaries shall not be able to gainsay nor resist." - Luke 21:15

Folks, the devil is a trickster, he will impose fear on you and fill your mind with doubts. It has been devil's winning strategy, so it is difficult for him to change it. He comes your way to magnify the battle or challenge, so that you will declare for him. Whosoever you support in the face of any confrontation wins the battle. The devil came to one of our patriarchs called Job, and he discovered that Job declared for God, then he threw in his jab (that is his winning strategy). Hear Job:

"For the thing which I greatly feared is come upon me, and that which I was afraid of is come unto me".

- Job 3:25

Your voice is the devil's main target in any battle of life, whether in the physical or spiritual realm. Fear is the devil's greatest weapon of attack. Fear of failure has kept many from attempting anything. Fear makes you break the hedge, and so contradict God's principle. The fear of failure can still make great men and women today not to attain anything.

"For as he thinketh so is he"

Proverb 27:3.

You can't think failure and command victory; you can't think like a peasant and rule in the palace.

Whatsoever that dominates your thought realm; that you portray.

Hear this:

"Hast not thou made an hedge about his house, and about all that he hath on every side? Thou hast blessed the work of his hands. And his substance is increased in the land". - Job 1:10

God always build a wall or hedge roundabout you but you can keep it or break it.

"He that diggeth a pit shall fall into it and whosever breaketh an hedge a serpent shall bite him." - Ecclisiastes10:8

There are deposits of creative power in you. The moment you get what the word of God said concerning your situation, faith is built up. The word conceived in your heart formed by the tongue and spoken out of the mouth becomes creative power that will work for you.

When Jesus spoke to the fig tree, there was no immediate manifestation of curse but later it came to pass. At the tomb of Lazarus, Jesus did not ask God to do the speaking for him. He addressed the dead body to come forth.

> **What you are today is a product of what you have said about yourself in the past**

"As in water, face answereth to face, so the heart of man to man". - Proverbs 27:19.

Therefore, the battle field that the devil fights hard to capture is your mind. Mind you, you don't win on the outside, until you win in the inside. Fear and doubt are subtle killers.

> **IF YOU CANT FIND YOUR PLACE IN THE SCRIPTURE, YOU WILL NOT FIND YOUR PLACE AMONG MEN.**

Chapter 2

POWER FOR WINNING

Winston Churchill said, "The Empire of the future will not be built on concrete, soldiers or iron gates, but rather the empire of the future will be the empire of the mind".

In the amplified version of the bible, Job 32:8 says *"There is a vital force in man, the spirit of intelligence but the inspiration of the almighty giveth them understanding"*. The word vital means essential or important. Therefore, <u>mind is an essential force</u>. It is a force that is required to win in any conflict. You don't win in the outside until you first win in the inside. **Mind is essential force**.

When God gets hold of people and fills them with the spirit, they can have a cry, a massage, and a proclamation of the gospel that will move others. Those who do not have the spirit of the Lord may cry for fifty years and see nobody take notice of them. There are three types of heart - the spiritual heart, the heart that connect with God; the biological heart - the heart that pump blood and the mental heart - the reasoning heart.

"A man's heart deviseth his way: but the Lord directeth his steps. - "Proverb 16:9".

The heart mentioned in this verse is the mental heart (the reasoning heart). Reasoning is process of making inferences through logical, rational and analytical thinking.

"Counsel in the heart of man is like deep waters; but a man of understanding will draw it out."

Proverbs 20:5.

What you need to excel in life is inside you. Your mind is extraordinarily a computer. Yet it works in a simple three-way step. First it takes in information that is what you see, hear, smell, taste and feel. Secondly it processes this information- How does what I sense relate to me? After processing the information, your brain tells you what action to take to handle it. For instance, if your mind tells you it is raining (information input). If you don't want to get drenched (information processed), you put on a raincoat (action of the processed information).

WHAT YOU ALLOW INTO YOUR MIND, AFFECTS YOU POSITIVELY OR NEGATIVELY.

A cliche of modern times often heard around people who work with computers is garbage in, garbage out" (the human mind is a prototype of a computer). Feed in wrong or bad data, the processed information will be misleading and vice versa. A key step in achieving more is to make sure the right information is fed into the mind for processing. Information is the taproot of bravery." The more informed you are, the most productive" so protect your mind, it is your asset in life.

"Keep thy heart with all diligence; for out it is the issues of life". - Proverbs 4:23.

Your mind is worth more than a million dollars. If you keep an amount worth millions, you will hire seventy men to guard that place.

But your mind is worth more than that. Your mind is the exclusive source of all you will create spiritually and materially in your life. Typically, people allow gossip, rumor news, scandals, murders, embezzlements, bankruptcies, bribery and other misceaneous negative information to enter their mental computer. For instance, the bad terrible world is coming to an end. Mind polluters come from two sources (a) people we associate with on daily bases, (b) the media. The end of December nineteen hundred and ninety-nine (1999), people nearly ate up what they had, believing the world was coming to an end. There was this rumor too, about the three orange men that appeared in Lagos, people concluded that the world has come to an end. Our beliefs affect our decision, our action and the direction of our lives.

"and nothing will be restrained from them which they have imagined to do." - Genesis 11:6b.

The word imagination means to form pictures in your mind. Imagination came from the word image. It is the ability to deal resourcefully with unusual problems. It is in fact, a thing of the mind. Imagination means to have mental pictures or to form mental images of a thing.

"And the Lord said unto Abraham after that Lot was separated from him, lift up now thy eyes and look from the place where thou act, north ward and west ward: for all the land which thou seest, to thee I will give it, and to thy seed forever.". Genesis 13:14-15.

It is your picture that determines your real future, you don't get what you are unable to behold. What you behold, you hold.

Imagination is the workshop of your mind. It is the factory where your future is framed before it comes into existence. For a religious mind, imagination will sound awkward but I want to say this, I don't pray for the future, I program into it. Everything you can see about your future God is committed to bringing it to pass.

"A man's heart deviseth his way. But the lord directed his steps." - Proverb 16:19.

A man who put his mind to work cannot be stopped. A man of imagination will soon arrive to his destination.

TOO MUCH ANALYSIS LEADS TO PARALYSIS.

Beware of professional advisers. Don't let them hinder you from your victory.

"And Simon answering said unto him, master, we have toiled all night, and have taken nothing; nevertheless, at thy word I will let down the net."

- Luke 5:5

Peter told Jesus, I know this profession very well, more than any other. It is unwise to fish in the day, it is better in the night season. We have done the normal thing and it yielded no result. He forgot that excuses limit ones potentials. ``but nevertheless at thy word'' ``the end of man's limitation is God's beginning'' in other words, "man's extremity is God's opportunity"

The counsel of Saul could have denied the shepherd boy (David) his victory.

"And Saul said to David thou art not able to go against this Philistine to fight with him; for thou art but a youth and he a man of war from his youth".

- 1 Samuel 17:35.

David knew the power of victory; "Declare thou, that thou mayest be justified". – Isaiah 43:26b

You can confirm by his declaration here;

"Though I walk through the valley of the shadow of death, I will fear no evil for thou art with me; Thy rod and thy staff they comfort me". Psalm 23:4.

He was conscious of divine presence. "Any time a man looks away from God, he starts to have problem". There is no shadow without a reflection of light.

Miracle in your mouth, your mouth is the principal requirement in the school of signs and wonders.

"A man's belly shall be satisfied with the fruit of his mouth and with the increase of his lips shall he be filled" - Proverb 18:20

<u>Your mouth is a vital tool for your required victory in all phases of life.</u> Without your mouth, your winning may take long. God said your mouth and the proper application of it when necessary will command your required victory.

"Say unto them, As truly as I live, saith the Lord, as ye have spoken in Mine ears, so will I do to you". – Numbers 14:26

During creation, there was darkness, confusion, the earth was formless and empty, and then God used the mouth tool and said "let there be light … and everything came to shape. Child of God, you can shape your world by using your mouth effectively.

"For I will give you a mouth and a wisdom, which all your adversaries will not be able to gain say nor resist."
- Luke 21:15

The Lord promised to give you a mouth and wisdom to use in any conflict which no enemy (opponent) can resist or contradict. David declared his victory before the fight. He spoke into the end before the battle began. He wasn't intimidated by the size of his problem or trouble (Goliath).

"David said that, the same Lord, who delivered him out of the paw of the lion and out of the paw of the bear, he will do it again" (paraphrased). 1 Samuel 17:37.

Folks, choose the right words, say it and you will have whatsoever you say.

"And now Moses said unto the Lord, O my Lord, I am not eloquent, neither heretofore, nor since thou hast spoken unto thy servant, but I am slow of speech, and of slow tongue. And the Lord said unto him, "Who hath made man's mouth? Or who maketh the dumb, or deaf, or the seeing, or the blind? Have not I the Lord? Now go, and I will be with thy mouth, and teach thee what thou shalt say" – Exodus 4:10-12

Moses, the anointed of God knows the danger of not being persuasive, convincing, articulate and expressive in your daily speeches.

Speak solutions and not the problems. This is the world's problem, which has also engulfed the church.

"How forcible are right words". - Job 6:25.

Nothing is as forceful as right words.

"A word fitly spoken is like apples of gold in pictures of Silver" Proverbs 25:11.

The right word at the right time is like a custom-made piece of jewelry. Therefore, with your words, belittle your enemy - Take the scriptures you know very well to challenge the situation confronting you. Let the word of Christ dwell in you richly in all wisdom (Colossians 3 vs 16a). Your enemy (the devil) is like a roaring lion, he is not the lion. Speak faith into all conditions. Give verdicts, I will never fail, I am a winner; I will make it etc.

Hear David:

"This day will the Lord deliver thee into mine hand, and I will smite thee and take thine head from thee, and I will give the carcasses of the host of the philistines this day unto the fowls of the air, and to the wild beast of the earth, that all the earth may know that there is a God in Israel". - 1 Samuel 17:46.

Make your boast in the lord. David trusted absolutely in the ability of God. Your victory is a product of your declarations. The victory you command today or what is happening today around you is a bye product of your lips. Words have special powers which creates smiles or frowns, the power to generate laughs or tears, the power to lift or put down, the power to motivate or de-motivate, the power to heal or harm. Choose your words carefully. Be careful with your words, once they are said, they can only be forgiven but not forgotten. Your mouth will determine what becomes of you. "More people are victims of their tongue than they are of the devil". Words from your mouth have both substance and influence. They can bring situation under control or escalate them. The more positive things you speak, the more good things you will have. If where you are is not good for you, speak what you want into the place.

"A man shall eat good by the fruit of his mouth".
Proverbs 13: 2a.

"He that keepeth his mouth keepeth his life".

Proverb 13:3a.

If you don't say the right things concerning your life, you will remain the way you are.

Your mouth is a vital tool for your required victory in the conflicts of life.

PREPARATION

"The preparations of the heart in man,
and the answer of the tongue
is from the Lord" - Proverbs 16:1

No one excels in life without exercise. Prayer is not a substitute to preparation and planning. Planning will rather stir you into preparation. <u>"Your level of preparation determines your level of attainment"</u>. No one becomes a champion inside the ring. It is your preparation that gives you confidence. Confidence breeds reward, but it is birthed by preparation. "The level of your preparation determines the level of your performance". <u>"The time to repair the roof is when the sun is shining"</u>. Many people emphasize on luck today, but luck is what happens when preparation meets opportunity. <u>Luck means labor under correct knowledge</u>". There is another type of luck (lock), labor outside correct knowledge. Success depends upon previous preparations, and without such preparations there is bound to be failure. There is no secret to success. It is the result of preparation, hard work and learning from past failures.

"If the iron be blunt, and he do not whet the edge,
then must he put to more strength: but wisdom is
profitable to direct"

- Ecclesiastes 10:10.

Jesus who is the duality of both divinity and humanity had to prepare for his ministry. He sat under doctors to hear them and to ask them questions.

"And it came to pass, that after three days they found him in the temple, sitting in the midst of the doctors, both hearing them, and asking them question and all that heard him were astonished at his understanding and answers". - Luke 2:46-47

"If you prepare well, you will amaze your world".

"And David put his hand in his bag and took there a stone". – 1 Samuel 17:49

Inside David's bag was a stone. He didn't pick the stone from outside. This shows that he was determined and ready for fight. He knows what he can do well, so he started with that. He was a specialist in stone throwing. <u>Do not be like mushroom which springs up overnight and disappears at the appearance of the sun.</u> Don't rush your destiny. Confidence is the conqueror's backbone; it is what makes you fit for the battle. It was Daniel's companion in the lion's den. You don't have much to offer without confidence. Folks, you have enough reason to be confident, because, "if the Lord be for you, no one can be against you". It is the secret of the game, and it destroys all opposition no matter how formidable.

A group of tourist were in a village in Umuaro (a town in Imo state – South East Nigeria), one of them asked an elderly man, "Has any great man been born in this village?" The old man replied, no, only babies". Every person who has ever achieved anything has struggled for it.

In 1936, Jessie Owens came back from the Olympic Games as the world's fastest runner.

At the huge press conference, the first question asked him was, "How did you do it, Jessie? Four gold medals, you embarrassed Hitler (the fastest man in the world) in his hometown, how did you do it?''.

Oh he said, "I think it all began when I was a kid back in junior high school, my coach got us together and made a speech I've never forgotten. The main thing he said was, you can pretty well become whatever you make up your mind to be.

Dreams never become realities unless you have the courage to build a ladder to them. You build ladder to your dream one step at a time. So as you are preparing please do quick to act. Remember procrastination is the fertilizer that makes difficulty grows".

Chapter 3

UNBEATABLE STEPS TO VICTORY

There are steps one need to take to lunch into his victory in life. These steps will work for anyone, anywhere at any time because they have root in God, and they are centered on God's word. The word of God does not know culture or geographical barriers. It is constant, it works if rightly applied. The success of your dream and your future lies on your ability to see beyond what is, to what will be.

> *Dreams never become realities unless you have the courage to build a ladder to them.*

"The poor and the oppressors have this in common; the Lord gives sight to the eyes of both"

Proverbs 29:13 NIV.

Oswald J. Smith said, "Eyes that see are common, but those that see vision are rare"

VISION

Helen Keller who, though blind and deaf achieved much said, "The greatest tragedy to befall a person is to have sight but lack vision". Do you know why Esau ate his birthright in a single lunch? He was a man who could not see beyond the present. He had no foresight. Jacob, on the other hand, saw the future and asked for the birthright.

"And Esau said to Jacob, feed me I pray thee with that same red pottage, for I am faint; therefore, was his name called Edom. And Jacob said; sell me this day thy birthright. And Esau said behold I am at the point to die; and what profit shall this birthright do to me. And Jacob said, swear me this day; and he swear unto him; and he sold his birthright unto Jacob. Then Jacob gave Esau bread and pottage of lentiles; and he did eat and drink, and rose up, and went his way; thus Esau despised his birthright". - Genesis 25:30-31

<u>Vision is the ability to picture your future from the scriptures as to feature in the future.</u> What visionless Esau despised, a visionary Jacob desired and demanded. A man of vision is a man who sees differently. A visionary Jacob saw an opportunity to take the birthright, what a visionless Esau could not see beyond pottage. A visionary invest in opportunities, the visionless squanders and wastes opportunities; <u>A man is not more than what he sees about himself.</u>

"And it came to pass, when they were gone over that Elijah said unto Elisha, ask what I shall do for thee, before I be taken away from thee. And Elisha said, I pray thee, let a double portion of thy spirit be upon me. And he said, Thou hast nevertheless, if thou see me when am taken from thee, it shall be so unto thee, but if not, It shall not be so.

2 kings 2:9-10

> When they reached the other side, Elijah said to Elisha, "What can I do for you before I'm taken from you? Ask anything." Elisha said, "Your life repeated in my life. I want to be a holy man just like you." "That's a hard one" said Elijah. " But if you're watching when I'm taken from you, you'll get what you've asked for. But only if you're watching." 2 Kings 2:9-10 MSG

Note that word, "Your life repeated in my life. I want to be a holy man like you. This is vision and he held to it and did not allow anything deter him from receiving it.

Already Elisha has made great effort in following his master beyond the Jordan. Even after asking for the double portion of his master's spirit which his master considered a hard thing to ask, he had one more hurdle to cross. Elijah told him," nevertheless if thou see me when am taken from thee, it shall be unto thee" Effort is good, just as Elisha made much effort. Prayer - oh yes he prayed hard, but beyond that he needed to see. <u>Hard prayer but poor sight might still keep you below the poverty level.</u> The way Elisha looked and eventually saw, you discovered that even his persistent determination and prayer were all fixed by vision.

> ***Vision is the ability to picture your future from the scriptures as to feature in the future.***

Vision is the act of seeing things invisible. Where there is no vision the people perish. The poorest man in the world is not the one without a kobo (money) but the one without a vision —Helen killer. <u>Visionary men are those on mission who understand their purpose and</u>

can define their targets. There is a zeal that runs a vision. Information is the raw material of vision, only people who look forward gets reward. Vision is that picture in your mind's eye that keeps you going when things get tough. Vision is supernatural insight on what God wants you to be. For a man to experience the supernatural, he must have a view of the supernatural realm. The ordinary human eyes do not see that far. Vision is the eye that sees things that are invisible. A man of vision must be a man of faith.

> **A man is not more than what he sees about himself.**

INFORMATION

Information breeds transformation. The beginning of any transformation is rooted on information. When you lack information, you can be called a foolish man.

"The labor of the foolish wearieth every one of them, because he knoweth not how to go to the city"
Ecclesiastes 10:15.

Information is the taproot of bravery. Labor without information culminates in foolishness. Your level of relevance is determined by the level of information you have. The most informed are the most productive. Every great destiny is rooted in information. Exploits belong only to the informed. All kingdom stars are secret hunters.

"As it was in the days of my youth when the secret of God was upon my tabernacle"

Job 29:4

"I Daniel understood by books." - Daniel .9:2.

Your insight determines your height in life. Testimony is divine information for transformation. Information is the currency of today's world. Those who control information are most powerful people on the planet earth and not ones with most bulging bank accounts. The timely delivery of vital information is one of the most lucrative businesses you can have in this new millennium. I should know. I started one of the most successful brokerage businesses in the country .I am also perhaps the world's most information broker, I have made millions of dollars from doing it, and am going to show you how to easily do the same. Let me backtrack a little bit. All my life I wanted to start my own business. I didn't care what it was, I just wanted to learn how to feed myself and not work for someone else. I even considered selling hot dogs on mall near the Washington monument. I just wanted to be my own boss. Sound familiar?

I had a string of failed businesses before I hit the big time. It was while working as a computer administrator of a travel company that I learned something that changed my whole life. The hot shots that ran the company fascinated me. They were powerful individuals who discussed and negotiated and executed big deals all the time. In order to get in on some of that wheeling and dealing, I would hang around late at night when they had their meeting and volunteer to get coffee and dough nuts, do the xeroxing -do anything to try to learn how to be like them. One day they came into my office and asked me- not to get coffee but to get information on how good or bad the rental car business was. It seems they were considering making a bid to acquire Avis Rent a car, and needed some good market information to go along with the financial statements, they were poring over. I, of course, said. "Yes, yes, yes!" I was their "yes man" even though I knew nothing about the rent a car business and had no idea where I was going to get this information. Well I wanted to do this so badly, I could almost taste it. This was one giant step up from coffee and xeroxing that lucky people are offered once in a life time, and I did not want to blow it. I saw myself as Young Turk on the way up the ladder of success. But I didn't have a clue where to go for the information. I sat in my little office wondering if I could make the grade. I sat there staring at my desk hoping something would pop into my head and give me the magic answer. I stared at the telephone and then picked it up thinking: Here I am in Washington D.C. needing to know about the rental car business. Who can I call? Why not the government? I pass all those big buildings every day on the way to work. Maybe someone there can help me, well it worked, by starting with the government information operator, I was able to work my way through a dozen more calls and referred in the rental car business. It turned out to be a man who used to be the president of hertz and was now in Washington - and bored out of his mind with this government Job. He actually invited me to lunch so he could tell me everything he knew. I was shocked, I couldn't believe that in 45 minutes on the telephone, I could locate a real expert who was willing to tell me everything I needed to know about the rental car business. And he even wanted to take me to lunch! Afterwards, I was so excited about the information I had just received that I burst into a meeting, my boss was having with his hot spot merger and acquisition buddies. He was eager to hear everything I learned from my lunch right then and there. They were blown away. They couldn't believe that a Young Turk like me 'who didn't know anyone,' could get such information that we had all assumed was privileged and confidential. I got more excited about the information I dug up on the rental car business than with any program ever wrote for the company I knew then that information was power. I also knew that there was immense value in delivering timely information. I was hooked, I started a new business obtaining information for people on anything they needed. I became a consultant to people in the merger and acquisition they needed to make their business a success - information they were unable to find themselves. This time, the business grew from just me, a telephone, and a desk in my one-bedroom apartment to over 30 employs as a million and half-dollars' sales in a little more than 3 years. Even after a string of failing business, I finally realized my first success and I will show you can do it too. How to create money out of thin air, what I learned earlier on is that you can literally take information that is free to obtain, but often times hard to find for average person to find – turn around and sell it for big bucks. All it requires is a little Resourcefulness and the knowledge of where to find the information that is sellable. There is nothing to it. These are the only things you need.

1. Believe on the notion that, we live in an information society, and if you're willing to make few necessary calls or e-mails, you can gather information on almost anything - and make that information sellable.

2. You need to know where to look for the information. Although there are countless sources of information, if you do nothing else but tap into the world's largest source of free information, you can find virtually everything that you need. That source is the U.S government. {I've spent 25 years of my life as an information broker and I am yet to find a source of information more comprehensive then the U.S government}.

Do you want to get an idea of just how vast the government information reserve is? If you took all the major commercial publishers in the United States, they collectively produce 50,000 new titles in all the libraries and book stores around the country in a single year. In contrast, one single publisher in the government (the national technical information service) publishes over 100,000 titles a year. Multiply that by the number of government agencies that produce information and the amount of information becomes absolutely staggering! The range of subjects on which you can find information is also mind–boggling. The government not only counts people, the number of jelly beans manufactured in the country, toilets installed, and how many potatoes grown; but also gives investment trends and opportunities likely to show up in the wall street journal in weeks; it also answers any legal question better than the highest paid lawyer. There are 700,000 government experts in any field you can imagine who will give you free information simply because you asked.

HOW TO USE THE INFORMATION YOU GATHER

1.   Find customers who need, and are willing to pay for, specialized information. Position yourself as

someone who knows how to find information on practically everything. Do narrow down the types of information you can get for your customer's specific needs. That way, you zero in with the precision of a sharpshooter, instead of just firing a shotgun that goes in all direction. As an information broker, always remember what Willy Sutton said when asked why he robbed Banks. He said "because that's where the money is" you need to have the same slogan if you want to stay in business. Choose the path of least resistance. Choose a customer base that consists of rich people or big companies that have money to spend by finding out how they can get richer and the ones that are willing and able to spend it.

Gather specialized information that would be of great interest to a specific business sector (example: internet marketers). Position yourself as an expert on a particular subject, then write in-depth special reports that feature the specialized information you found, package them in an e-book, and make them available to internet marketers for a fee. As an alternative, you may also create newsletter that regularly updates the specialized information on the paid subscriptions. More and more businesses are realizing the value of having good information for good decision-making whether big or small, a business can't succeed today unless it keeps the latest information. What kind of information do businesses need? They need information on their markets, their competition, technology, money sources and regulations, for starters. Develop sensitivity to the needs of your prospects by asking them directly what they need. From that, you can determine the kind of information that would best satisfy their needs. Here is a useful tip:

You would do well to develop a "hook" a hook is a marketing term that makes it easier for people to purchase your services. It is taking the situation I mentioned earlier about "knowing how to find information about practically anything" and refining it down to a specialty. If you specialize in some interesting aspect of the information brokerage industry, it is easier to attract your prospect's attention. Define your reach by identifying the customer group that you specialize in helping: small businesses, or non-pro-organizations. Or you can define it by the area of information you want to deal with, such as health information, company information. Another way you can describe your business is by the medium of the information you provide, such as: only database searches, only document retrieval, or only interviewing industry experts. I was fortunate enough to have started in Washington D.C, where I developed the hook of government information. It gave me an instant edge over my competitors, even though I had no more experience gathering information than they did. To make a long story short, the government information I have amassed over the years have earned me a coveted position of being a New York times syndicate columnist, and I have even authored two New York times best-sellers featuring information that I have obtained for free. I have also been privileged to be regularly featured as the nation's top expert on government information on TV programs such as Larry king, David Letterman, Jay Leno today show and Good morning America. The key to becoming a successful information broker is first to find the information and deliver it on time to those who want it, then sit back and watch the money appear out of the thin air.

PLANNING

Planning is God's optimal solution for winning in life. It is a proper arrangement of things in order for action. Planning is God's wisdom secret for increase in productivity. If you don't have a program, you won't experience progress. Planning cures disorder. Failure to plan is planning to fail. I have found this to be true, therefore I do plan for every step I take.

"Any enterprise is built by wise planning; it becomes strong through common sense. It profits wonderfully by keeping abreast of the facts".

Proverbs 24:3-4 TLB.

This is why I read, listen to messages, study and dialogue with friends. I want to reduce the surprise factor as much as possible. Life itself presents enough surprise even for thoroughly planned people. Therefore, when you fail to plan in one area, you have set yourself a potential failure in other areas as well. Organize your vision into believable steps.

"And the lord answered me, and said, write the vision and make it plain upon tables, that he may run that readeth it". - Habakkuk 2:2

The word make it plain means to crystalize it. "Don't think your vision, ink it". "A faintest line is better than the strongest mind". Write your thoughts, crystallize your thinking which in turn prompts you to action. "A short pencil is better than the longest memory". If you want to succeed, you must plan your work. Remember, Planning takes time, discipline, courage and patience but profits wonderfully. Whatever you can't measure, you can't monitor. If you want to be successful,

You must plan your work and work your plan. Order is the mother of progress.

"A wise man looks ahead". Prov. 14:8 (TLB).

"We should make our plans counting on God to direct us. Prov. 16:9" (TLB).

<u>Planning is the medium through which you translate opportunities into possibilities.</u> You stop winning when you stop planning. It is a non-transferable responsibility. It is planning that gives life to your resources or your pursuit.

"Moreover the profit of earth is for all: the king himself is served by the field." Ecclesiastes 5:9.

There was a young man; he has no name, the Bible called him - The prodigal son.

"And when he came to himself, he said how many hired servants of my father have bread enough and to spare and I perish with hunger". - Luke 15:7.

> **"Whatever you can't measure you can't monitor".**

The prodigal son started all again through the act of reasoning. Folks, you can still make it. His reasoning metamorphosed into planning. You have no problem until you have someone to blame for it. The man at the pool of Bethesda lacks planning and celebrated 38th year anniversary at the pool close to his miracle. It is possible to waste a whole life time if you don't plan. Listen, many substitute prayers for planning. Therefore, reasoning is the proper raw material for result oriented progress. A mystical approach to progress will make you miserable citizen on earth, as many business men and women are not planners, but carriers of talisman and woman.

THE RULE OF THE GAME

God wanted everyman to be responsible that is why He introduced work. He gave man the ability to do everything but it is unfortunate that at the Garden of Eden, Adam became irresponsible. <u>Responsibility means to respond to your ability</u>. What was given to Adam, he let the devil stole it from him. Work is not a curse; it is God's plan for man, what people call LUCK means labor under correct knowledge

NOTE: The word "LABOUR".

"And the Lord planted garden eastward in Eden; and there he put the man whom he formed. And the Lord God took the man and put him into the Garden of Eden to dress it and keep it. - Gensis2: 8; 15.

The man was placed in Eden to be its gardener, this was before man's fall. So work is part of mans' living.

"Go to the ant thou sluggard; consider her ways, and be wise which having no guide overseer or ruler, provideth her meat in summer and gathered her food in harvest. How long will thou sleep O sluggard? When wilt thou arise out of thy sleep? Yet a little sleep, a little slumber, a little folding of hands to sleep; so shall thy poverty come as one that travelleth and thy want as an armed man". - Prov. 6: 6-1 1

> ***Planning is the medium through which you translate opportunities into possibilities.***

<u>SLUGGARD</u>

This is a lazy individual who refused to work and whose desires are not met. This is an idle, slothful person

"... And hard work will get everything he wants". -
Proverb 13: 4 (GNB)

Go to work so that you can get up to the world. Stop sleeping away your destiny. The more you sleep the more tired you become. Repetition they say, is the mother of skill.

"Jesus answered them, my father is always working and I too must work". - John 5: 17 (GNB)

> ***Responsibility means to respond to your ability***

Remember serving takes effort, When God wanted sponges and oysters, He made them and put one on a rock and the other in the mud when he made man, he did not make him to be spongy or an oyster; he made him with feet and hands, head and heart and vital blood; and placed him in Eden and he said to him go work.".

> ***"The harder the work, the better the product".***

Chapter 4

HABITS OF CHAMPIONS

Great men and women only possess great habits. Every man's future is traceable to his daily routine. Joseph saw his future through dreams and today he is the world most successful prisoner. Progress involves risk, he who does not dare, will not get share. Jesse Owens said, there is something that can happen to every athlete, every human being – it is the instinct to slack off to give in to pain, to give less than your best, the instinct to hope to win through luck of your opponents, not doing their best instead of going to the limit and pass your limit where your victory is always to be found.

"And David left his carriage in the hands of keeper of the carriage and ran into the army and came and saluted his brethren. And as he talks with them, behold there came up the champion, the philistine of Gath, Goliath by name of the armies of the philistines and spoke according to the same words and David heard them and the children of Israel when they saw the man, they fled from him and were so afraid. And the men of Israel said have ye seen this man that is come up? Surely to defy Israel is he come up and it shall be that the man who killeth him, the king will enrich him with great riches and will give him his daughter and make his father's house free in Israel".

1 Samuel 17: 21-22.

WILLINGNESS TO GROW INTO GREATNESS
It is not where you started, it is where you finished that counts, nothing lasting in life starts from the top. The only venture that starts from the top is the grave. As small acorn grows into a great oak tree, so grows the seed of greatness within our lives. David has been training in the secret before he came to the open. No one excels in life outside exercise.

"Though thy beginning was small, yet thy latter end shall greatly increase" - Job 8:7

Every great thing begins small. Never despise your beginning in life, God has a beginning.

"In the beginning." - Gensis1:1

Therefore, by all means, try something. So many gigantic businesses today, started small. Champions in various fields started small, little is much when you commit yourself to it. Growth in life begins with decision as decision is your pathway to honor. Never you be like mushroom that spring up overnight and disappear at the appearance of the sun.

TIME MANAGEMENT
The more you control your time, the more you will be in control of your life. Almost everyone complains about not having enough time yet the way many people act shows they place almost no value on their time. Any social business day is a business failure. The loss of gold is more, the loss of honor is much, they can be recovered, but the loss of time is much more because time lost can never be regained. Plan the use of time as well as money. Time is an interruption in eternity.

It is the most precious gift God gave to man. You may delay, but your time will not. People complain about lack of time, It is not lack of time that is their problem, it is lack of direction and planning.

"Seeing his days are determined the number of his months is with thee, hast appointed his bounds that he cannot pass" - Job 14: 5.

Treat time with the wisdom it deserves, determine what you want to accomplish each day (daily to-do list) set a deadline for attainments. Avoid time wasters, bored friends, and unnecessary phone calls. You have time enough if you will but use it aright.

LISTENING

David heard all that the philistine (Goliath) said and also heard what the reward is like. And he said, this opportunity will not pass him by. The first step to winning is the willingness to listen.

"The hearing ear, and the seeing eye, the Lord had made even both of them." - Proverbs.20:12.

One sentence can be golden key to the next season of your life. Learning is the pathway to living. What influences your life comes from hearing.

In Mark chapter 4 verses 23 and 24, Jesus declared:

"If any man has ears to hear, let him hear". Take heed, what you hear".

The measure of thought and study you give to the truth you hear will be the measure of virtue and knowledge that comes back to you. To hear is very strong, but beware of what you hear.

What you hear has positive or negative influence over your victory in life. You cannot have a positive life with a negative mind.

TAKE MASSIVE ACTION

Procrastination is opportunity assassin. Take massive urgent action. Action is the fertilizer of faith. Thank God for your faith, but if there is no action it is dead.

"And it came to pass when the philistines arose and came and drew nigh to meet David that David hasted and ran towards the army to meet the philistine."

1 Samuel 17: 48.

Make a plan, plan to work and work your plan. Don't dream about what you will plan to do, don't just talk about what you plan to do, don't just write down what you plan to do - take action. Nothing in life jumps on us, No one jumps on your bandwagon until you get it going. **When you move, your mountains are removed.

"Laziness lets the roof leak, and soon the rafter begin to rot." - Ecclesiastes 10:18(TLB).

ATTITUDE IS EVERYTHING

Expect the best and you will get it, expect the worse you will get it equally. Your mental attitude determines your outcome (altitude).

"And the lord said behold the people is one, and they have all one language and this they began to do and nothing will be restrained from them, which they have imagined." - Genesis 11: 6.

Expectation always gives birth to experience. As a man thinketh so is he. Therefore, it is our nature that determines our actual future. How you think now or what is in your mind, determines the result you command. Folks, what's in your mind? Champions are wonderful thinkers. Edison said; ''some men think in words but he said he thinks in pictures''. It is your picture that determines your real future. Please mind what you think. Think success and you will have it.

"Finally brethren whatsoever things are true whatever things are pure, whatever things are lovely, whatever are of good report if there may be any virtue and if there be any praise think on these things."

Philippians 4:8.

Our thinking attitude must be focused on true, pure, just, lovely and honest things not to be negative at all on anything. If we can hold unto this scripture, then we have got to experience a real future.

<u>COURAGE</u>
"Be strong and of good courage".

Joshua 1:6b.

Desire is your wish bone; courage is your backbone. Your backbone gives you the courage, the get-up-and-go, the guts to achieve, the incentive to make any dream you dare dream come true. Courage precedes great activity; courage precedes decision making. The greatest risk in life is, not having the courage to go for our dreams. All promises minus courage amounts to nothing. Anytime courage dries up, failure sets in.

Men of courage never looks on who supports them, they see great opportunities at all times. Courage is the ability to resist obstacles, with the belief of reaching your desired goal. Courage magnets divine assistance, enables one announce his victory before the fight and is the conquerors' backbone.

"And Saul said to David. Thou art not able to go against this philistine to fight with him, for thou art but a youth, and he a man of war from his youth. And David said unto Saul, thy servant kept his father's sheep and there came a lion and a bear and took a lamb out of the flock; And I went after him, and smote him, and delivered it out of his mouth: and when he arose against me I caught him by his beard, and smote him and slew him. Thy servant slew both the lion and bear and the uncircumcised philistine will be as one of them."

1 Samuel 17: 33-36.

David had courage to persist and press forward, the professional's council from General Saul notwithstanding 'For thou art but a youth'. Please don't destroy yourself, keep your zeal, it is good to attempt, but not in this one. Goliath is a man of war from his youth, this council could silence any person but Courage will ignore it. No one becomes a champion outside of contest. For one to accomplish any task, he must summon courage. No courage, no accomplishment".

In 1903, The Wright brothers in North Carolina, USA successfully flew the first powered metal which lasted for only one hour against heavy oppositions that no metal can fly. Courage is what it takes for any exploit.

Nothing will ever be attended if all possible obstacles must first be overcome. Out of every crisis creativity is born. The Bible said, David put his hand in his bag and brought out a stone. Courage empowers any man. You need it, go for it.

It is not strange that we fear that which never happens; that we destroy our initiative by the fear of defeat when in reality defeat is the most useful tonic and it should be accepted as such.

CONCENTRATION

Concentration is not a faculty of the mind but it depends on the control of attention.

"Brethren, I count not myself to have apprehended: but this one thing I do forgetting those things which are behind and reach forth unto those things which are before, I press towards the mark for the prize"
Philippians 3: 13-14a.

It is easy to concentrate when everything is going great. Champions are the ones who concentrate when defeat is staring them in the face. Concentrate hard on your goals. Your entire worrying and complaining are not going to change what happened five minutes ago. You can only change what will happen next. Focus on that, don't look back, and don't brood. Focus your concentration on what you can do now and forget the past, it simply does not exist anymore.

HANDLING CRITICS

If you are successful, people will be jealous and criticize you. Don't let them distract you from reaching your goal.

When people throw stones at you, it is because you are a good tree full of fruits. There are lots of harvest in you. Don't go down to their levels by throwing back the stones on them, but throw on them your fruits so your seed might inspire them to change their way. <u>It is easy to criticize other people but it is hard to duplicate their effort</u>. Never hate people who are jealous of you, but respect their jealousy. They are people who think that you are better than them. Critics are not doers or leaders in life. The leaders and doers are very busy with their own accomplishments.

"And Eliab his eldest brother heard when he spoke unto the man and Eliab's anger was kindled against David, and he said, why comest thou down hither? And with who hath thou left those few sheep in the wilderness? I know thy pride, and the naughtiness of thine heart; for thou art come down that thou mightiest see the battle. And David said what have I now done? Is there not a cause?".

Samuel 17:21-29.

Champions follow one course until they become successful. They focus on their purpose in life. David was on course and the critics against him did not stop him. These characterizes the life of champions.

> *"It is easy to criticize other people but it is hard to duplicate their effort".*

Chapter 5

ACCEPT RESPONSIBILITIES

Responsibility is the price one pays or must pay for greatness. No irresponsible person will ever become great. It takes discipline to be distinguished. Irresponsibility dethrones people, it robs covenant children of their covenant rights. You can't go behaving like a child and expect to be enthroned. <u>If you don't accept responsibility, you will die a liability.</u>

"Now I say that the heir as long as he is a child, differeth nothing from a servant, though he be lord of all. But is under tutors and governors until the time appointed of the father." - Galatians. 4:1, 2.

> ### If you don't accept responsibility, you will die a liability

There is no way God can enthrone a child to the throne who cry every second, pointing accusing finger at one person or the other for his mistakes. God doesn't experiment and He is not a wicked God. He would not place glory on you that is more than what you can handle. Indiscipline is the major problem of many Christians. Unemployed Husbands and wives owning two cars with their legs crossed at home watching television, this is total madness. Why should a man wake up in the morning and not know what to do?. Indiscipline disqualifies any covenant child from becoming a champion.

David, our example in this book learnt constantly in the secret place, he is in the stone throwing business that is why he got his target (the face of Goliath) though thoroughly covered.

You don't become a champion by wishing, you become a champion by training. Do you know why Adam failed? He was mistakenly created an adult. The day he was born was the day God started talking to him. He was given responsibilities before he learnt responsibility. <u>Whatever you don't make, you cannot keep. Whatever you have not earned, you can't sustain. You must accept responsibilities before you will experience reality,</u>

<u>INVEST IN YOURSELF</u>

Life is not only a gift, it is an investment,

"But through knowledge shall the just be delivered."

Proverbs 11:9b

Knowledge is power, and information is the taproot of bravery.

"If you faint in the days of adversity, thy strength is small. A wise man is strong; yea a man of knowledge increases strength." - Proverbs 24: 5 and 10.

This therefore means that your strength for conflicts is tied in your skill. Skill is the product of knowledge<u>. Skill is the factory where success is manufactured</u>. Most people do not take time to invest in themselves until there is an emergency. It is vital to prepare before challenges come.

In fact it is essential you invest in yourself for improvement. Investment in your mind is the best investment you can ever make in the world.

Once you gain knowledge, no one can steal it away from you. Personal growth and self-knowledge promotes self-confidence and belief. Once you have self-confidence and belief, you will be unstoppable. Knowledge is mostly gained by reading good motivational books, listening to anointed tapes, messages and attending seminars organized by people who you look up to as mentors. Richard Branson read a book called 'Small is beautiful' and it turned him from a vendor to a chairman of virgin Atlantic airline. Get your mind to work, Dr David Oyedepo said; "Ask me what I do, I read and I think". No wonder he is doing exploits in every sphere. "My people are destroyed because of lack of knowledge." Hosea 4:6a

Being a child of God alone does not guarantee your victory. You need personal knowledge of what God says concerning your situation that alone will make you a victor instead of a victim. The right kind of information gives you the ability to see things correctly and put you in agreement with truth. ** Every good action produce a habit and habits decide the future. **The difference between men is not in their dressing, but in their habit.

<u>MOTIVATION</u>

Motivation comes from within. Self-motivation is essential to begin the path to the top. Enthusiasm and motivation takes you to the starting line and it is self-motivation that takes you beyond the finishing line and then to the top.

"Declaring the end from the beginning, and from ancient times the things that are not yet done, saying my counsel shall stand I will do all my pleasure."
Isaiah 46:10.

Keep a clear vision of your destiny and be inspired by the prospect of the result. Motivation keeps you going when sometimes the going gets tough. The fastest way to get motivated is to dream. Dreams are the raw materials for success. Get a dream and make a decision to achieve that dream. Personal breakthrough in life starts with a change in your beliefs. Blessed is he who expects nothing for he shall never be disappointed. Motivation is the inner strength that pushes you toward taking action and making achievements. It is powered by desire and ambition. Motivation is one of the most important keys to success. When there is motivation, you attain better and greater results and when you lack it, you get no result. Lack of motivation means lack of enthusiasm, zest and ambition. Whereas the possession of motivation is a sign of strong desire, energy and enthusiasm and the willingness to do whatever it takes to achieve what one set out to do. How to keep yourself motivated.

> *"Skill is the factory where success is manufactured".*

Visualize your goals as achieved, adding a feeling of happiness and joy. Constantly affirm to yourself that you can and will succeed. Set a goal, if you have a major goal. Have a mindset that whatever you start you have to finish.

Avoid procrastination: It is the fertilizer that makes difficulty grow. Read about subject of your Interest. That will keep you on the track. Look at pictures of things you want to get, achieve or do. It will strengthen your desires. Never give up. Keep the flame of motivation burning.

> **"The difference between men is not in their dressing, but in their habit"**

You grow like the company you keep. Associate with motivated people who share your interest. Socialize with achievers and people of similar interest or goal. Attitude is very contagious. Association transfers covenant.

"And when they came thither to the hill, behold, a company of prophets me him, and he prophesied among them. And it came to pass, when all that knew him before time saw that, they said; behold, he prophesied among the prophets, then the people said one to another, "What is this that is come unto the son of Kish? Is Saul also among the prophets?"

1 Samuel 10:10-11

STUDY SUCCESSFUL PEOPLE

Just as Like begets like, success breeds success. You will always grow like the company you keep. Walk in the steps of someone who has gone ahead of you and achieved what you want. If you stand on their shoulder you see clearer than they do. There are highly successful business men who have reached the top by studying the business from the masters that worked before them. Watch them, observe the way they work, the way they develop their attitudes, focus, vision and passion, and then emulate them. Association with successful people will empower you. You will begin to believe in yourself and in the possibilities of achieving your dreams and goals, ** If you fail to understand the footsteps of giants you will die a dwarf. ** Learn from David, he left the wilderness, and ran into the army to salute his brethren. Become a more focused person, follow one course until successful. The kind that others will like to be around. If you do what champions do, you will get their results.

> **"Blessed is he who expects nothing, for he shall never be disappointed"**

LEARN FROM FAILURE

Your past is over just as yesterday is over. Everyone makes mistakes, learn from your past mistakes because no one is perfect. Mistakes are the essential qualities of a man. If you have failed, learn from it because failure is a learning experience. "Failure is simply opportunity to begin again, this time more intelligently" - Henry Ford. Know that your tomorrow is full of promises. The most successful people in life are not those who failed the least, they are rather people who fail more because they try more. Champions are those who learn from their mistakes and never quit. Champions never let obstacles in life steal their dreams. You have seven allowances to fall and rise according to the scripture.

"For a just man falleth seven times and riseth up again." - Proverbs 24:16a.

"Rejoice not over me oh mine enemy: when I fall I shall arise." - Micah 7:8.

"The steps of a good man are ordered by the Lord, and delighteth in his ways. Though he falls, he shall not utterly be cast down: for the Lord upholdeth him with his hands." - Psalms 37:23-24

<u>Failure may look like a fact but it is just an opinion.</u> Successful People believe that mistakes are just feedbacks. Let failure motivate you and not paralyze you. If you have failed in any venture before, find a business you believe in and start all over again. Champions believe in a new beginning.

OPTIMISM

Optimists see the glass half full not half empty. Optimists know that tough times never last but tough people do. Optimists know that they are going to handle fascinating people, difficult people, people who reject them, people who are not easy to go along with and much more. When things go wrong as they sometimes will, when you want to give up and quit, get optimistic about the future and stay focused, do not be distracted by the naysayers. Optimism does not mean that your climbing to the top will be perfect. It means that you can imagine getting there and can visualize yourself already there.

"Know ye not that they which run in a race run all, but one received the prize. So run that you may obtain. And every man that strived for the mastery is temperate in all things" - 1 Corinthians 9: 24 - 25.

Optimism gives the hope of a fabulous future in the face of uncertainty. Go ahead attempt the impossible and succeed far more often than you would think.

"But Caleb reassures the people as they stood before Moses. Let us go up and possesses it he said, for we are well able to conquer it" - Numbers 13: 30 (TLB).

> ***Failure may look like a fact but it is just an opinion***

Caleb is a different kind of man. The Bible said that he had another spirit in him. That is the spirit of optimism. Beholding obstacles and interpreting it into opportunity.

CONCLUSION
DECISION: THE PATHWAY TO POWER.

Every man's progress begins with a new decision. The Lord will provide us with shovel, but we have to do the digging. Every decision culminates in choosing what is right for you. It is in the moment of decision that your destiny is shaped. What you decide on determines your testimony. Take a chance.

"And there were four leprous men at the entering of the gate: And they said one to another why sit we here until we die? If we say we will enter into the city and we shall die there, and if we sit here, we die also, Now, therefore come and let us fall unto the host of Syrians, if the save us alive we shall live and if they kill us we shall but die."

2kings 7: 3 - 4.

The four lepers changed their world by their decisions. The worthless men in the society, the relegated people of the world changed their fortune by their decision. You can change yours also. Assumption is the real mother of frustration. Stop playing it safe and go for greatness. Jesus told Peter to lunch into the deep for treasures are not on the surface. Your biggest failure, may lead you to your greatest success. Every great destiny is a child of great decision. When opportunities knock, pay attention. Risk is the game of success. Take risk to find out if you are on the right path. Sometimes you will succeed, sometimes you won't, but if you don't take action on opportunities, for sure, you will not succeed .There are opportunities everywhere, you alone are responsible for creating your own future. Luck is spelled work, when opportunity presents itself go for it, don't wait. One of the lepers asked, why sit we here till we die? Let us take urgent action now. If you wait, you waste. Every single event in life, however troubling or difficult, conceals opportunity. David saw Goliath as opportunity to change his status and he maximized it. The next is yours.

BE PERSISTENT

Success or failure in life is up to you. Don't blame others for your situation; you are responsible for what happens to your life. It's the sets of sails and not the wind that blows people off course. Champions outline circumstances, challenges and setbacks. Setback makes room for come back. Success doesn't come overnight. It takes persistence to become a champion.

Pressure separates the average competitors from a champion. Champions learn how to handle pressure. When pressure mounts; champions level it, because they are being tested,

All of us do well when things are going well but the things that distinguish champions is the ability to do well persistently in times of great stress. Folks follow these steps and you will automatically become a champion. YOU WILL MAKE IT!

SUCCESS MANUAL

All that mankind has done, thought or been is lying as a magic preservation in the pages of books.

The wisdom book of the Bible Proverbs 11: 9b said, "But by knowledge shall the just be delivered." Great men expose themselves to great books and great people that is what makes them great.

Daniel said *"he understood by books"* (Dan. 9: 2).

One's future in life is determined by the kind of friends and books he keeps or reads. You therefore grow like the company you keep. The easiest way to became truly useful is to seek the best that other brains have to offer. Success takes work and discipline, proper nurturing, and time which may not happen overnight.

There are two ways to learning:

Experience: Learning by your own mistakes.

Wisdom: Learning from the mistakes of others for wise is the man who learns from the mistakes of others.

Your existence is evidence that this generation needs something that your life contains.

A relaxed attitude lengthens a man's life.

A man may ruin his chances by his own foolishness and then blame it on the Lord or devil.

All the creative force starts with the word.

Action is the fertilizer of faith.

Anyone can start, but only the thorough bred will finish.

A man may accomplish almost anything today, if he just sets his heart on doing it and let nothing interfere with his progress.

A winner is he who gives himself to his work, body and soul.

An intellectual is a man who taken more words than necessary to tell more than he knows.

A borrower is a servant to the lender

Amazing changes in life are by-products of great decisions.

A leader is born when destiny is discovered.

Anytime you don't have light (word of God) activities are handicapped.

Any social business day, is a business failure.

Anytime you obey God, you create a season for success for yourself.

As long as a man controls your knowledge base, he controls your entire future.

Bible is God's manual for maximum result.

Bad news makes failure of any child.

Birds of the same feather fly together except eagles. Therefore, if you want to soar like the eagles learn the act of separation.

Brilliant ideas without hard work is a daydream.

Believing a solution paves the way for solution.

Bible is a book of pictures. It gives you a picture of God, a picture of the devil and God's photograph of you.

Be more concerned with your character than with your reputation. Your character is what you really are while your reputation is merely what others think you are.

Beware of little expenses. A small leak will sink a great ship.

Become a part of someone's miracle and it will come back to you.

Communicate everything to God, but only what edifies to others.

Concentration is not a faculty of the mind but depends on the control of attention

Crisis is not failure; it is only a process.

Confidence is a promoter of excellence

Challenges are the catalyst for your change.

Do not consume your tomorrow's feeding on your yesterday.

Discipline is the soul of an army. It makes small numbers formidable, procures success for the weak and esteem to all.

Distance is never measured in miles, but always by affection – never abandon a friend.

Depression is a trap of the enemy for captivity.

Dreams of the future are more valuable than histories of the past.

Discovery is the different between a failure and a winner.

Don not look on things as they are, but as they ought to be.

Dreams are the raw materials for success.

Discipline is the chief destroyer of waste.

Do not let what you cannot do interfere with what you can do.

Dreams inspire creativity in money management.

Don not raise money raise men and you will have more money than you ever think.

Discouragement is failure's partner.

Do not be deceived, there is seedtime and harvest time.

Don not allow your future to be unnecessarily predicted by imaginary factors.

Dreams are fulfilled only through action, not through endless planning to take action.

Excellence in any art is attained only by hard and persistent work

Every rising in life, starts with sitting.

Except you say 'I am', nobody says 'you are'.

Excellence is to do common things in an uncommon way.

Every man is ordinary, but if you want to be extraordinary, you have to do extra.

Every enterprise is built by wise planning it becomes strong through common sense. And it profits wonderfully by keeping abreast of the facts.

Every great investment had a small beginning.

Every person who has ever achieved anything has stretched for it.

Every great destiny begins in a certain day.

Every unwise activity leads to captivity.

Excuses limit one's potential.

Facts fuels faith and faith moves God. Therefore, it is the level of the information you carry that determines your future in life.

Faith is not a pill you take but the muscle you use.

Funds come from friends.

Forgiveness is always a gift. Forgiveness can never be

earned. It can only be given as is God's forgiveness to us.

Faith is the raw material that produce the substance that you hope for.

FOCUS: Follow one course until successful.

Failure to prepare is preparation for failure.

Failure is the opportunity to begin again more intelligently.

Faith is the reality of things at a distance that human eyes can't see.

God is more concerned with where we are going than where we are coming from.

Giving is never a magical solution to our problem.

God always looks at the finished product.

God can create something out of what seems like nothing.

God is your source of worth and wealth.

God's word is your blueprint for success.

God's pattern for success is a pattern of purification.

Goals are simply checkup points on the way to the dream of purpose.

Genius is only the power of making continuous effort.

God gives all things to industry, therefore plunge deep while sluggards sleep, you shall have corn to sell and to keep.

Godly exercise is the pathway to a dignified Christian life.

Get down to work so as to get up to the world.

God holds answer to every question of life. That is why he is beautiful for situations.

Great men and women simply have great habits.

God gave us firstly – information and secondly power. Freedom lies in knowing the truth.

Good-luck happens when opportunity meets with preparation.

God's secret will make star of any dummy.

Great men expose themselves to great books and great people. That's what makes them great.

Great ideas usually result from combinations of related information

Happiness, wealth and success are by–products of goal setting; they cannot be the goal themselves.

Harvest pattern is - condition the soil, sow the seed, water it, and then reap the harvest.

Heaven doesn't operate a lottery - give and hit a jack pot.

Humbling precedes blessing, as before honor is humility.

Honor lost is much, and can be regained, money lost is more and can be regained. But time lost is much more and can never be regained.

Honor comes only to those who try.

He who masters his time, has mastered his life.

It is not what you have, rather what you do with what you have that makes all the difference.

If you are doing your best, you will not have time to worry about failure.

It takes some will-power and persistence to train yourself to concentrate. But once acquired, it is one factor that will help your studies.

It is easier to obtain than to maintain.

If you sow daily, you will reap daily. It is the law of cause and effect. For every action, there is a reaction. Whatever you sow that's what you will reap.

Impression without expression leads to depression.

If you are a schemer like Jacob, you will soon meet with Laban.

It is a biblical law that you cannot get more than your eyes can catch.

In the race of life, only those behind sees how the ones in front are running.

If you don't want to be back bitten, then get behind.

If you don't want to be pulled down, then choose to be on the ground.

Information breeds confidence, go for it.

If you fail in times of adversity, your strength is small. A wise man is strong and a man of knowledge

increaseth strength.

In the multitude of counselors there is safety.

Insight is the tap root of bravery.

If you don't have a program, you won't experience progress.

If you don't know the value of time, you are not born for fame.

Ideas are the hardest currency in the business market.

Joy is the ventilator of the mental faculty.

Just as forgiveness opens relationships, so giving opens blessings.

Joy is the shock absorber of the vehicle of life.

Knowledge brings responsibility.

Knowledge alone gives big head but understanding gives you big heart.

Knowledge is the number one requirement in any conflict of life.

Life's greatest wealth is not in the money, but in friendships.

Life's greatest poverty is not in riches, but in spirit.

Luck is not a native of any country, LUCK simply means Labour Under Correct Knowledge.

Life is a race, therefore give it what it demands.

Life's great opportunities often open the road for daily duties.

Let yesterday's problems die with the dusk. If it does not, tomorrow's achievement and opportunities will not rise with the sun.

Listen to this: it takes two differences to agree.

Leaning is the pathway to maximum impact.

Life is not a matter of luck, it is a matter of light (knowledge).

Life is not measured in duration, but in donation.

Lack of Capital is not your problem rather lack of ideas.

Life demands best service often.

Leaders select their dreams and set their goals.

Man's extremity is God's opportunity.

Marriage is God's wisdom secret for man's dominion.

Man is made great or little by his own will.

Monuments are not to be built in the cemetery, but on the mind of those who you effected their lives positively.

Many are free from physical slavery, but not free from mental slavery.

Money does not make people but training because skill brings success.

Men are God's method, therefore, face life challenges, He is always with you.

Money flows to good ideas.

Make excuses for the shortcomings of others if you

wish. But hold yourself to strict accountability, if you would attain leadership in any undertaking.

Nothing that has come to you in life comes to stay, it all comes to pass.

No matter how often defeated, you are born a victor.

Never plant the seed of the past in the new field of relationship.

Nothing becomes dynamic until it first became specific.

Nothing will move until you move it. Remember the 2nd law of motion.

Nothing cheap carries value.

Nothing will be attempted if all possible obstacles first be removed.

Nothing in life has meaning except the meaning you give it.

No one wins a price without a payment.

Nothing great is ever attained overnight. It is one step per time.

Our financial battle is won by seed sowing, not at the bank, not with sponsors.

Opportunities never come to those who wait.

Out of every adversity comes an equal or greater opportunity.

Obedience to the word of God is the backbone for breakthrough.

Our vision in life always limits God's performance.

Orderliness is the guarantee for progress.

Only thinkers become stars. For when you stop thinking, you start stinking.

One man with courage makes a majority.

One piece of information can turn your struggle into success.

Purity is best demonstrated by generosity.

POOR means: Passing Over Opportunities Repeatedly.

Prosperity is the natural sequentially ordered result of righteousness in life.

Praise is faith in action.

Procrastination is an ingredient for difficulty.

People and devil will try to discourage you, but you and God are able to work wonders together.

Planning is the starting point of any dream.

Put the word of God first and everything will begin to work.

Persistence and determination alone are omnipotent.

Praise is a spiritual weapon against the odds of life.

Planning is God's wisdom secret for increase in productivity.

Productivity depends on your ability to set up a list of daily task in order of importance and accomplishing them.

Productive listening (paying attention to details) is vital for success.

People will surely criticize you if you have big dreams and ideas better than theirs.

Progress is like a wheelbarrow, if you stop pushing, it stops.

Quality decisions attract divine backing.

Repetition is the senior brother of skill.

Real faith will refuse to see anything that is contrary to the scripture.

Right words spoken are forceful.

Risk is the game of success.

Remember that need is the mother of creativity.

Society may predict, but only you determine your destiny.

Success can be reduced to a formula and failure can be reduced to a formula too. Apply the one and avoid the other.

Successes are usually scheduled events.

Success is achieved by those who try, for there is nothing to lose by trying and great deal to gain if successful, by all means try.

Some people's skyscrapers are in their stomach.

Success is making a continuous progress.

Success takes work and discipline, proper nurturing,

and time, and may not happen overnight.

Smile adds value to your face.

Skill is the principle factor in the school of success.

Timing is the essential ingredient in success.

The title you wear is not as important as the task you accomplish.

The weakening pills of men are women as the weakening pills of women are money. But whosoever is free from these things is wise.

The harder the training the better the product.

The secret of success is constancy to purpose.

The harder one works, the luckier one becomes.

Too much analysis always leads to paralysis.

The place of agreement is the place of power.

The darker the night, the brighter the light.

The brighter the light, the darker the night surrounding it.

The word of God is the heavenly prescription for right living, right thinking and right action.

The truth of God is the only thing you should allow to dominate and guide your life.

The only person that can stop you from what God intended for you is you.

Time is one of the most important ingredients in any

success formula for any human activity.

The future belongs to those who believe in the beauty of their dreams.

The brighter your light, the faster the journey.

There is no product without a process.

The lighter you are, the higher you fly. Psalm 119 v 130.

There are two essentials in life: what you believe and what you do.

The poor and the rich man have this in common - The Lord gives sight to the both.

The most powerful gift God gave you is the gift of choice.

The price for your health has been paid. So you can only take delivery of them on the pages of the scriptures.

The secret of your future is hidden in what you do daily.

The greatest weapon of the devil against any enterprise is division.

The Bible law of progress is one step after the other.

The world says, seeing is believing but faith says believing is seeing.

The depth of your love determines your height in life.

Try not to become a man of success, but rather try to become a man of value.

The best legacy you can bequeath a child is education.

The only success without hard work is the dictionary definition of success.

The moment great leaders lack, frustration takes over.

The best way to knowing a way is to make enquiry.

The most informed are the most productive.

There are no hopeless situations, there are only people who think hopelessly.

There is one guaranteed formula for failure that is, trying to please everyone.

The talent God gave you is what you need for initial take off then you go and build it.

There is no future in any career, the future lies in the one holding it.

Thomas Edison said, someone asked him how he gave the world so many inventions. He said, because I never think in words, I think in picture. Genesis 13 vs. 14, 15.

The work of God is finished, but your faith is under construction. Num. 13: 30.

Talent without skill equal to trash.

There are two forces that build the gigantic machine called credibility which opens the door to success, trustworthiness and expertise.

The man who expects great things makes noble plans and daily pursues them, cannot help but succeed.

The mind must first see the visual achievement of purpose before action is initiated.

You are a sum total of what you think Prov. 23: 7.

Vision is the blueprint on the inside of a leader before ever the plan on the outside.

Vividly imagine, sincerely believe, ardently and enthusiastically act and it must inevitably come to pass.

Vision is that picture in your mind's eye that keeps you going when the going gets tough.

Worry is a route which leads from somewhere to nowhere. Don't let it direct your life.

Where you are is not as important as who you are.

We leave the old and enter the new by way of crisis.

When your mind is reconditioned by God's thoughts, you can see the possible instead of the impossible.

Will is the power of self-direction.

Work is the time secret of life.

Word reading and prayer is the divine prescription for radiance.

Wealth is a product of man's capacity to reason.

Where you refuse to change, you end-up in chains.

When you miss your location, you will miss your allocation.

Wisdom is using the available to get what you require.

Where there is unity, you pray less and things work of its own accord.

Wisdom is better than weapons of war.

What determines your manifestation is your expectation.

Words have both substance and influence. They can bring situations into control or put them in disorder.

Write your thoughts, crystallize your thinking which in turn prompts you to action.

Character is a perfectly educated will.

Character is the foundation of a worth- while business.

Character is who you are in the secret.

You can't be bitter and be better.

Your first step to changing your destiny is knowing the promises of God for you.

You are a poor specimen if you can't stand the pressure of adversity.

Your understanding of the scripture is the gateway to your destiny.

You can't reach your destination taking another man's route.

Your exploit is hinged upon your understanding of the word of God.

Dan. 11: 32.

Your future depends on many things but mostly on you.

God can use you right where you are today. God uses willing vessels not brimming vessel. Throughout the Bible in order to fulfill his plan for the earth, God used many people from all works of life. **He used**:

Aaron, a servant, who became God's spokesman.

Abraham, a nomad, who became the father of many nations.

David: A shepherd boy, who became a King.

Deborah: A housewife, who became a judge.

Elijah: A homely man, who became a mighty prophet.

Esther: An orphan, who became a queen.

Gideon: A common labourer, who became a valiant leader of men.

Hosea: A marital failure, who prophesied to save Israel.

Jacob: A deceiver whose name became Israel.

Jacob: A refugee, who became the father of the twelve tribes of Israel.

James and John: Fishermen, who became close Disciples of Christ and were known as "sons of Thunder"

Jeremiah: A child, who fearlessly spoke the word of the Lord.

John the Baptist: Vagabond, who became the fore runner of Jesus

Joseph: A prisoner, who became a prime minister.

Joshua: An assistant, who become a conqueror.

Mary: An unknown virgin, who gave birth to the son of God.

Moses: A slaughterer, who become a deliverer.

Nicodemus: A Pharisee, who became a defender of faith.

Paul: A prosecutor, who became the greatest

missionary in history and author of two-third of the New Testament.

Peter: Who denied Jesus thrice, but became a great evangelist of his time

Shadrach, Meshach, and Abednego: Hebrew exiles, who became great leaders of the nation of Babylon.

Be the whole person God called you to be. Don't settle for anything less. Don't look back. Look forward and decide today to take steps towards God's plan for your life. Believe in yourself, all things are possible with God.

The End.

Thank you for having this book. I believe the knowledge and information contained in this book has greatly inspired you.

Contact the Author: Jeff Raymond Ukah.

Email: alpharay4real@gmail.com

Phone: 08033777894

www.ingramcontent.com/pod-product-compliance
Lightning Source LLC
Chambersburg PA
CBHW020747160726
47993CB00006B/2649